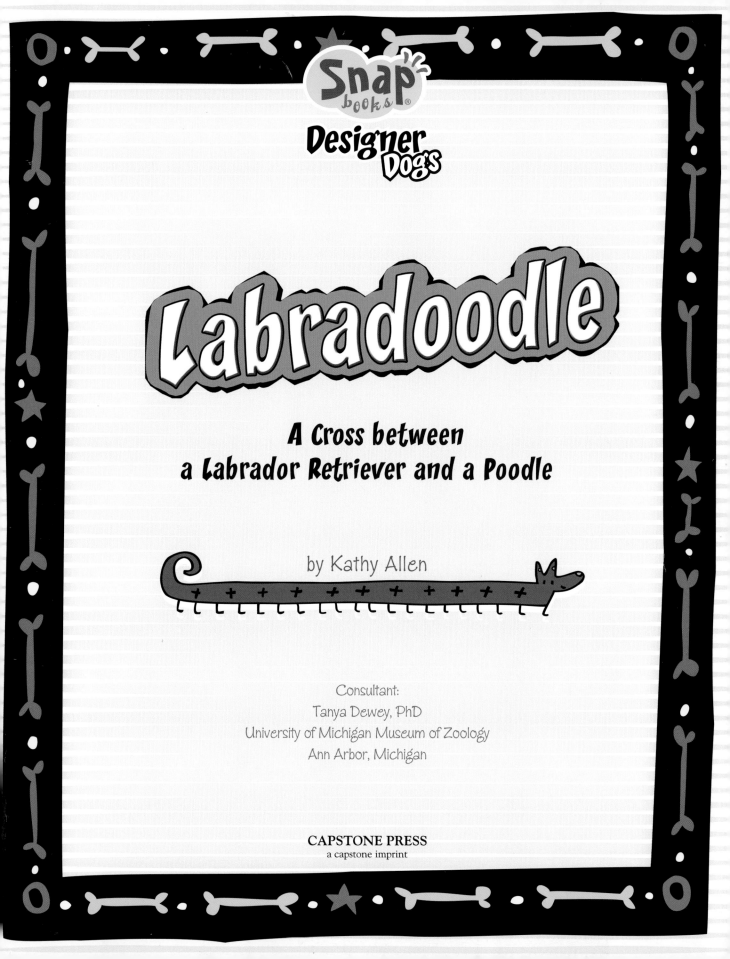

Snap books®

Designer Dogs

Labradoodle

A Cross between a Labrador Retriever and a Poodle

by Kathy Allen

Consultant:
Tanya Dewey, PhD
University of Michigan Museum of Zoology
Ann Arbor, Michigan

CAPSTONE PRESS
a capstone imprint

Snap Books are published by Capstone Press,
1710 Roe Crest Drive, North Mankato, Minnesota 56003.
www.capstonepub.com

Books published by Capstone Press are manufactured with paper
containing at least 10 percent post-consumer waste.

Library of Congress Cataloging-in-Publication Data
Allen, Kathy.
Labradoodle : a cross between a Labrador retriever and a Poodle / by Kathy Allen.
    p. cm. — (Snap. Designer dogs)
Includes bibliographical references and index.
Summary: "Describes Labradoodles, their characteristics and behavior, and includes basic information on feeding,
grooming, training, and healthcare"—Provided by publisher.
ISBN 978-1-4296-7666-3 (library binding)
1. Labradoodle—Juvenile literature. I. Title.
SF429.L29A45 2012
636.72'8—dc23

2011036703

Editorial Credits
Editor: Lori Shores
Designer: Veronica Correia
Media Researcher: Marcie Spence
Photo Stylist: Sarah Schuette
Studio Scheduler: Marcy Morin
Production Specialist: Kathy McColley

Photo Credits:
Capstone Studio: Karon Dubke, cover (bottom right), 5, 7, 8 (right), 9, 13, 15, 23, 25, 26, 27, 28, 29; Shutterstock: Basheera Designs,
16, Erik Lam, cover (bottom left), 8 (left), Ersin Kurtdal, 19 (top), Gary Paul Lewis, 21, Joy Brown, cover (top), 18, Steven Belanger,
19 (bottom), Studio1One, 11, Wendy Meder, 17

Printed in the United States of America in North Mankato, Minnesota.
062012   006797R

Table of Contents

Chapter 1

Designer Doodles

There's a dog you may not know at the local dog park. It often has a coat of striking curls. It loves to play with other dogs. It may bound up to you and flop over for a belly rub. What is this bubbly dog turning heads around town? It's a Labradoodle. The name may sound silly, as many designer dog names do. Also called a Doodle, the Labradoodle is a cross between a Labrador retriever and a Poodle.

Behind the shiny curls and the silly name is a dog that does some serious work. Because doodles are smart and loyal, they make great assistance dogs. Assistance dogs help their owners with day-to-day living. Some of these dogs guide the visually and hearing impaired. Other Labradoodles bark to alert when an owner is about to have a seizure. That's one smart pooch!

WHAT IS A DESIGNER DOG?

Designer dogs aren't **purebred** dogs, but they aren't mutts either. A mutt is a dog that comes from parents that are mixes of different breeds. Mutts are usually unplanned combinations. Their parent breeds aren't always obvious. A purebred dog comes from two parents that are also the same purebred breed. A designer dog is neither of these. It is a cross of two different purebreds.

People began breeding designer dogs in the 1980s. Some designer dogs are bred to avoid health problems. Breeders hope that crossing two purebreds will prevent health problems common to the parent breeds. Others designer dogs are bred to avoid shedding for people with allergies. But some designer dogs are bred simply to be good pets.

Dog Fact!

For the special edition of Monopoly: Here and Now, the Scottish Terrier game piece was replaced with a Labradoodle.

purebred—having parents of the same breed

Join the Club!

According to the American Kennel Club (AKC), a purebred dog comes from a long line of the same dogs. Purebreds should look and act like their parents. But designer dogs don't always look or behave the same way. For this reason, the AKC doesn't recognize designer dogs as true breeds. Some breeders are working to create a standard Labradoodle to be considered as a purebred. In the meantime, there are groups that help breeders and teach the public about Labradoodles.

- Labradoodle Association of Australia
- International Labradoodle Association
- Australian Labradoodle Association of America

A Chorkie is a cross between a Chihuahua and a Yorkshire Terrier.

Chapter 2

Meet the Parents

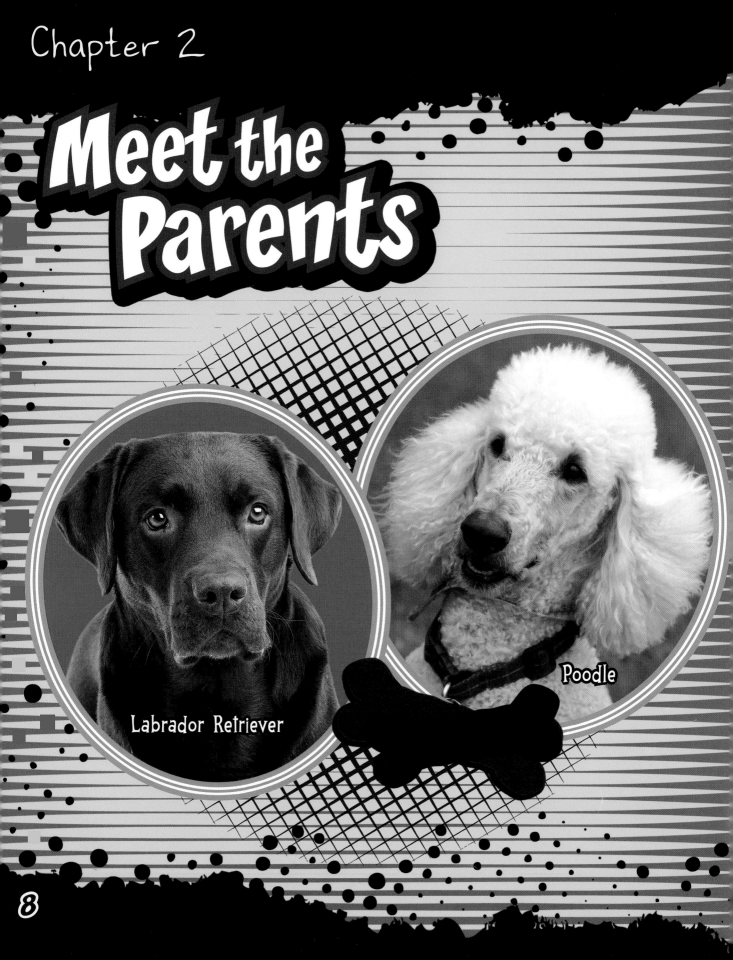

Labrador Retriever

Poodle

Getting to know a mixed-breed dog begins with learning about its parents. Whether it's a designer dog or a mutt, a little research will help a lot. Mixed-breed dogs can have any combination of their parents' **traits**. Knowing the parent breeds' traits will help predict how a puppy will behave.

The Labradoodle story begins with an Australian woman who needed an assistance dog. Because of her allergies, she could not have a dog that sheds. Popular assistance breeds, such as the Golden retriever, would not work for her. Right away a breeder named Wally Conron thought to cross two purebreds, and he had just the dogs in mind.

Dog Fact!

The Labradoodle was the first designer dog.

trait—a quality or characteristic that makes one person or animal different from another

POODLES

Conron began with the Poodle. Poodles are smart, loyal dogs that happily work for their owners. They are active, energetic, and easy to train. Poodles have long been popular hunting dogs. Their water-resistant coats shed very little or not at all. For this reason, the Poodle is ideal for people with allergies.

Poodles may be three sizes—standard, miniature, or toy. The standard Poodle can be more than 15 inches (38 centimeters) tall and weigh 45 to 70 pounds (20 to 32 kilograms). Toy Poodles are under 10 inches (25 cm) tall and weigh only 6 to 9 pounds (2.7 to 4 kg). No matter their size, the Poodle's beauty and grace make it an eye-catching pet. They are one of the most popular breeds for pet owners.

Dog Fact!

Poodles get their name from the German word for "puddle dog." They were bred to bring back birds from lakes and ponds for their hunter owners.

LABRADOR RETRIEVER

Labrador retrievers are also a favorite with pet owners. Despite their large size, Labs are gentle dogs. Loyal and sensitive, they're good pets for families with children of all ages. They learn tricks and earn praise easily. They're smart and trainable like Poodles and make excellent assistance dogs. Some Labs even have jobs with police departments as **detection dogs.**

Like Poodles, Labs are athletic dogs. They keep active playing fetch or hunting with their owners. Labs even have webbed paws, which makes them good swimmers. Their bodies are strong and muscular with short, straight hair. Their yellow, black, or brown coats are water-resistant like the Poodle's coat. Unlike poodles, however, Labs shed. Hip and knee problems are also a concern with these large dogs.

detection dog—a dog that is trained to find explosives, illegal drugs, or blood

Mix it Up!

Poodles and Labs are not always the only breeds in a Labradoodle's family tree. Some breeders include Irish water spaniels or cocker spaniels in their breeding. Crossing these breeds with the Labradoodle creates a softer, thicker coat that does not shed.

Chapter 3

Beauty and Brains

Today Labradoodles are one of the most popular hybrids. Owners say these dogs are a joy to be around. As pets, Doodles are gentle, which makes them good companions for kids and other animals. Because some Labradoodles are large dogs, they may accidentally play too rough. Owners should always supervise play between large Doodles and small children.

Labradoodles are social and intelligent dogs. They are good with new people and other dogs. These dogs enjoy spending time with their families. Owners say that their Labradoodles will play happily for hours. Doodles' intelligence and need to please make them easy to train.

A Labradoodle's size depends on what kind of Poodle parent is used. In general, Doodles come in three sizes, just like Poodles.

- standard—21 to 24 inches (53 to 61 cm) tall
- medium—17 to 20 inches (43 to 51 cm) tall
- miniature—14 to 16 inches (36 to 41 cm) tall

miniature

standard

Miniature Doodles can weigh as little as 15 pounds (6.8 kg). Standard Doodles weigh as much as 65 pounds (29 kg). Their ears lie flat on their heads, and their eyes are wide. The Labradoodle's tail is set low and sometimes curls. Doodles are light on their feet and graceful. Overall, the Labradoodle has the look of a friendly, charming dog.

Labradoodles can have one of three different coats—hair, fleece, or wool. A hair coat is straighter than the others. It sheds, so it is not the coat most breeders hope for. Fleece coats are soft and silky. Some doodles with fleece coats shed, but many do not. The wool coat is most like a Poodle's thick, curly coat. It doesn't shed, so it's perfect for people with allergies. The three coats can also be curly, wavy, or straight.

Like the Poodle's coat, Labradoodles' coats are great in the water. They're not completely waterproof, but they do shed water. Their coats also protect them against very hot or cold temperatures. No matter what type of coat they have, Labradoodles can be many colors. Most Doodles are black or a golden tan. Doodles can also be red or brown.

hair coat

fleece coat

wool coat

19

Chapter 4

Doodle Dos and Don'ts

Is the friendly Labradoodle the dog for you? If so, finding your Labradoodle starts with finding a good breeder. Labradoodle associations are good places to start. Local veterinarians might be able to recommend good breeders as well. Animal shelters may also have Labradoodles you can adopt. Shelter dogs have often been **spayed** or **neutered**. They are also less expensive than dogs from a breeder.

spay—to operate on a female animal so it is unable to produce young
neuter—to operate on a male animal so it is unable to produce young

Stay Away from Puppy Mills

Being popular is not always a good thing for a dog. Some people breed and sell as many dogs as they can for profit. These breeding operations are known as puppy mills. The dogs are not provided with proper medical care and living conditions. Puppies are raised in cramped, dirty spaces and often have medical problems. Good breeders have large, clean areas for their dogs. They will also show you proof that a puppy's parents are healthy.

21

Caring for a Labradoodle begins at the veterinarian's office. The vet will give your dog **vaccinations** to keep it healthy. The vet will also prescribe medicine to keep your Labradoodle safe from heartworms, fleas, and ticks. Yearly visits to the vet will help keep your pet healthy.

The vet can also help you decide what type of food will be best for your Doodle. Good quality food will keep your dog running and playing. You can feed a Doodle dry food or a mix of dry and wet food. Puppies need to eat often and should have food made for young dogs. An adult Labradoodle should eat twice a day. If your dog needs a special kind of food because of age or allergies, the vet will help you choose one.

vaccination—an injection or dose of medicine that protects a person or animal from disease

Grooming is a big part of caring for a Doodle. Labradoodles should be brushed once or twice a week. Doodles with hair coats may need more brushing because they shed. Labradoodles should be bathed about once a month with shampoo made for dogs. Bathing too often can dry out your dog's skin.

Labradoodles also need care for their teeth and ears. Brush your Labradoodle's teeth daily with dog toothpaste. Be sure to also check your Doodle's ears during grooming sessions. The inside of a Labradoodle's ears can get dirty. Their ears need regular cleaning with a solution sold at pet stores. Your veterinarian can show you how to gently clean your dog's ears.

Exercise is key to raising a healthy dog. Labradoodles have a lot of energy to burn. They need to be walked every day. In addition to exercise, walks provide entertainment for dogs. Dogs have a strong sense of smell. On walks, they can sniff around to find out who else has been out walking. Doodles are smart and curious dogs. Without regular activity, they will get bored.

Labradoodles also love to play. Playing fetch is a great way to have fun with your dog while providing good exercise. And don't forget that both Poodles and Labs are water dogs! Not all Labradoodles enjoy swimming but many do.

Training a Labradoodle

Training is one of the best things you can do for your dog. Both Poodles and Labs are intelligent dogs that train easily. Doodles are easily trained because they want to please their owners. The best way to train any dog is to have a clear routine that stays the same from day to day. Start with basic commands, such as "sit" and "stay," that will keep your pet safe and in control. Once basic training is done, you can also teach your Doodle tricks. From shaking hands to catching a Frisbee, training your dog will be quality time for both you and your pet.

Is a Labradoodle the right dog for your family? Or would a Lab or Poodle fit better in your home? Now that you know what to expect, you'll have an easier time choosing. No dog is perfect—not even one designed to be! But training and proper care can help any dog become a cherished member of the family.

Should You Adopt a Labradoodle?

Answer the following questions. The more "yes" answers you have, the more likely a Labradoodle is right for you.

1. Is someone in your home during the day to keep your dog company?
2. Do you have time to walk your dog every day?
3. Do you have time to groom your dog every week?
4. Do you have the patience to train your dog?
5. Do you have the time to check shelters or research breeders?

Glossary

designer dog (di-ZINE-ur DOG)—a dog created by breeding two purebred dog of different breeds

detection dog (di-TEK-shuhn DOG)—a dog that is trained to find explosives, illegal drugs, or blood

neuter (NOO-tur)—to operate on a male animal so it is unable to produce young

purebred (PYOOR-bred)—having parents of the same breed

spay (SPAY)—to operate on a female animal so it is unable to produce young

trait (TRATE)—a quality or characteristic that makes one person or animal different from another

vaccination (vak-suh-NAY-shuhn)—an injection or dose of medicine that protects a person or animal from disease

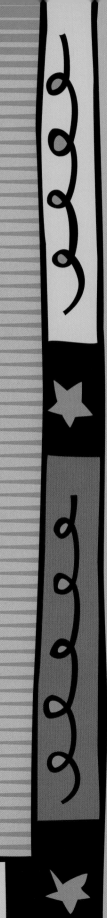

Read More

Bennett Woolf, Norma. *Hot Dogs! Fourteen of the Top Designer Dogs.* Hauppauge, N.Y.: Barrons, 2007.

Larrew, Brekka Hervey. *Labradoodles.* All About Dogs. Mankato, Minn.: Capstone Press, 2009.

Stone, Lynn M. *Labradoodles.* Eye to Eye with Dogs. Vero Beach, Fla.: Rourke Pub., 2009.

Internet Sites

FactHound offers a safe, fun way to find Internet sites related to this book. All of the sites on FactHound have been researched by our staff.

Here's all you do:

Visit *www.facthound.com*

Type in this code: 9781429676663

Index